The World
AEROBATICS
CHAMPIONSHIPS

The World
AEROBATICS
CHAMPIONSHIPS

Don Berliner

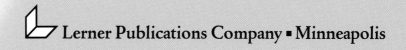 Lerner Publications Company ▪ Minneapolis

To the memory of Harold Chappell

All words printed in **bold** are explained in glossary on p. 60.

Cover photo and photo on page 47 courtesy of the U.S. Aerobatic Foundation. All other photos by Don Berliner.

Library of Congress Cataloging-in-Publication Data

Berliner, Don.
   The world aerobatics championships/Don Berliner.
    p. cm.
   Includes index.
   Summary: Follows pilot Debby Rihn as she trains for and participates in the 1986 world championship for aerobatics, the modern version of airshow stunt flying.
   ISBN 0-8225-0531-2
   1. Stunt flying—Juvenile literature. 2. Stunt flying— Competitions—Juvenile literature. [1. Stunt flying. 2. Rihn, Debby.] I. Title.
TL711.S8B48   1989   88-18128
797.5′4—dc19   CIP
                                        AC

Manufactured in the United States of America

1 2 3 4 5 6 7 8 9 10 99 98 97 96 95 94 93 92 91 90 89

CONTENTS

Pilot Debby Rihn brings her light, maneuverable aerobatic airplane in for a smooth landing.

INTRODUCTION

In western Virginia, the peaceful hills of the Shenandoah Valley echoed with the roar of an engine. All alone in the sky, a miniature red and white **biplane** (a plane with both upper and lower wings) twisted and turned and doubled back on itself. Inside the cramped cockpit, the pilot strained to fight off the pull of six times the force of gravity. Blood rushed to the pilot's head and quickly back down toward her feet.

It looked for all the world like a World War I dogfight, except that there was not another airplane anywhere in the sky. The battle was between the pilot and perfection, for the goal of the flight was to fly maneuvers without a single flaw. The pilot was struggling to fly loops that were absolutely round and rolls that ended within 1° of where they should. In a few weeks, the world's toughest critics would be staring at her airplane, ready to deduct valuable points for the tiniest error.

The game was **aerobatics**, a modern, sophisticated version of old-time air-show stunt flying. Today's competition aerobatics is a sport of people and machines working together in close harmony. The competitors are amateur sports pilots who see in this special branch of aviation an opportunity to put their minds and bodies into a quest for perfection. These pilots train for years to fly a four- or five-minute series of complicated maneuvers without a single flaw. The sport requires pilots to face

great mental strain and physical punishment; the reward is mostly one of personal satisfaction.

In order to fly the toughest sequences of maneuvers known to aviation, these skilled pilots need some very special airplanes. Over the years, aerobatic airplanes have evolved into the most nimble and powerful small craft imaginable. The airplanes and their pilots must withstand heavy pressures called Gs, or **g-forces**—similar to the pressures put on a car rounding a sharp curve—that alternately stretch and crush them. The airplanes are smaller than the typical two-seat personal plane, yet they are twice as powerful and four times as sturdy. Because they are for sport, rather than for travel, aerobatic planes lack many of the common comforts. They are noisy and cramped, too hot in the summer and too cold the rest of the year.

Together, the pilot and the airplane can do things otherwise impossible in flying. What they can do is so exceptional that an aerobatics World Championship has been held every two years since 1960. Each Championship year, the finest aerobatic pilots from all over the world gather in Europe or North America to fly their hearts out. Judges on the ground stare at a plane's every motion, grading its pilot against perfection.

In world competition, pilots are judged in four stages of competition: the **Known**, **Freestyle**, **Unknown**, and **Four-Minute** flights. Competitors receive individual points (and medals) for these stages, and the pilot with the most individual points becomes the new World Champion. The team whose pilots together outfly and outscore all other teams brings home the Nesterov Trophy.

In the first World Championships, pilots from Eastern Europe—Czechoslovakia and the Soviet Union, in particular—dominated the sport, using the best airplanes and the most intensive training. In the years following, the U.S.A., Czechoslovakia, and the Soviet Union have all shared honors.

1
TRAINING THE U.S. TEAM

The pilot in the sky was Debby Rihn (pronounced REEN), one of the nine pilots on the 1986 United States aerobatics team. Rural Virginia was the American training ground for the Thirteenth World Aerobatics Championships to be held in South Cerney, England.

The week of practice flying in Winchester, Virginia, was designed to prepare the pilots to face the best competitors from more than a dozen other countries. The U.S. team had chosen Winchester because of its similarity to the site of the World Championships. Not only was the airfield just as flat, but there was even a slightly curving road on the east side of the aerobatic flying zone, just like the one that would be used for orientation in England. The team met and worked in hangar space provided by famed Jaguar race car driver, Bob Tullius, who lives in Virginia.

Everything possible had been done to simulate the real competition. A judge on the ground noted each little flaw in Debby's maneuvers, and a video camera recorded the entire flight so that she and the judge could review it immediately after her landing. They would study each maneuver, point out the mistakes, and discuss how best to correct them the next time she flew. Judges stood at the corners of the 1,000-meter-square **aerobatic box** to

Debby was selected for the U.S. team because of her high finish in the previous year's National Championships at Denison, Texas. The top five women and the top five men in the Unlimited class (the most expert level) at Denison got the big prize: a trip to Europe to represent their country. There were only four women on the 1986 team because the fifth had just gotten a new job and couldn't get the necessary six weeks of vacation. Members of the U.S. team receive no pay for representing their country, though their living expenses are paid by the U.S. Aerobatic Foundation.

Debby Rihn was the favorite to lead the American women in their bid to upset the long-dominant Soviet women's team. (Only in the World Championships are the standings of men and women kept separately. All contestants, however, fly the same maneuvers in the same airplanes.) In the last Championships, held in 1984 in Hungary, Rihn had surprised everyone by placing third and winning the bronze medal in her rookie year. Her scores, combined with those of fellow pilots Linda Meyers and Julie Pfile, had earned the U.S. the silver medal in the Women's Team Championship.

record each time she flew out of bounds. The "box" is a "playing field" of air, directly above the airport, inside of which a pilot must perform all maneuvers. Judges with sighting wires watch to make sure the invisible boundaries are observed. In the Championships, flying out of the box would cost Rihn hard-earned points.

In her daily life, Debby was a licensed flight examiner. She was qualified to give tests to prospective pilots and was co-owner of a flying school in LaPorte, Texas. Prior to 1984, she had been a medical technologist, but she became so busy with her flying that she did not have time for both.

Debby's airplane for the 1986 competition was a **Pitts Special** S-1S, a single-seat two-winger small enough to fit into the average living room. It had a wing span of 17 feet, 4 inches (5.3 meters). The Pitts was 15 feet (4.6 meters) long, about the same as a full-size station wagon. It weighed less than 800 pounds (360 kilograms) when empty (no gas, no oil, no Debby). Debby's plane was built in 1979 for Chipper Melton, who flew it in the 1980 World Championships. It differed from the standard Pitts in many ways: it was designed to pass more smoothly through the wind, it had a bubble canopy over the cockpit, and its four-cylinder, air-cooled Lycoming engine could reach at least 200 horse-power (149.2 kilowatts).

Debby's counterpart on the men's team was Kermit Weeks, a veteran of four World Championships and a U.S. National Champion. Weeks had placed second among the men in 1984 and was a member of the reigning U.S. World Champion team. Previously, he had placed sixth in 1982 in Austria, third in 1980 in Oshkosh, Wisconsin, and second in 1978 in Czechoslovakia.

Once Debby and Kermit and the rest of the U.S. team got to Winchester, 75 miles west of Washington, D.C., they put all thoughts of their normal lives aside. This was the time to concentrate on aerobatics. Every day, each of the nine pilots flew three 15-minute practice routines. Forty-five minutes of strenuous aerobatics in one day is about all anyone can take and still remain sharp and alert and able to learn quickly. It is a demanding sport, both physically and mentally.

When a pilot was not flying, he or she had many other things to do. Flying sequences had to be put together, studied, and memorized. The airplanes had to be kept in near-perfect condition. Since the planes took as much of a beating as the pilots, daily inspections and frequent minor repairs required a great deal of time. The team included three full-time mechanics whose job was to get the airplanes into top shape and keep them that way.

Debby's modified Pitts Special had more than its share of aches and pains at Winchester. Its troublesome engine baffled the experts. A subtle combination of problems kept chief mechanic Ray Williams concentrating on Debby's airplane, tuning the engine, running it on the ground, and then fiddling with it in the air.

What bothered Debby's airplane bothered Debby. "I was really frustrated with all my maintenance problems. The airplane had given me so much trouble that I was a little concerned about it. Not that it was going to quit, but just the idea that it had kept me away from practice for a few days."

Pilots flew hard, and then they watched their teammates fly. Little by little, the group of skilled individuals became a team. Only during international competition is there such a thing as an aerobatics *team* in the U.S. The pilots normally train and compete alone. But now they noted flaws in one another's flying. Some of the mistakes were so small that only another top aerobatic pilot could see them. The pilots talked over problems they had performing individual maneuvers. The more experienced pilots such as Kermit and 61-year-old Henry Haigh, who was going into his sixth World Championships, tried to help the newer pilots prepare for a contest so very unlike any in the U.S.A.

In short order, the town of Winchester adopted the U.S. aerobatic team as its own. The team accepted invitations to dinner and to swimming pool parties as a way to meet the citizens and as a way to get a break from days of nothing but aerobatics.

But it was quickly time to move on to the United Kingdom. The training had gone better than expected. The pilots and airplanes were operating near top form. The team said goodbye to Winchester and to Bob Tullius, whose hangar had been their daytime home and whose wonderfully equipped shop had provided much-needed tools and expertise.

Residents of Winchester, Virginia, enjoy an aerobatic show—a parting gift from the U.S. team.

From the rear, one can see clearly the delicate tail equipment that makes the Pitts an excellent stunt plane.

Debby's Pitts and Kermit's Solution wait on the grass during a team meeting.

2

OFF TO BRITAIN

On Saturday morning, July 19, the U.S. pilots left Winchester for Dover, Delaware—the pilots in their nine little airplanes, the **groundcrew** in Bob Tullius's two private airplanes and in personal cars. The next major leg of the journey was underway, and it would be a long one—3,700 miles (5,953 kilometers). To prepare for it, everyone gathered in a huge hangar at Dover Air Force Base, almost on the Atlantic shore. Dover is one of the busiest bases in the U.S. Air Force's Military Airlift Command (MAC). Quartered there are some of the largest air transports ever to fly, among them the C-5 Galaxy cargo planes.

It would be one of these massive, camouflaged cargo planes that would carry the entire U.S. team across the Atlantic Ocean to England. At 2:50 P.M., Debby and her teammates began pushing the nine tiny airplanes into the huge, open nose of the military transport. It was a lot like pushing them into a hangar

for the night, except that this hangar was the cargo hold of an airplane! The storage space was so large that most of the aerobatic planes went straight in.

After traveling from the U.S. to England, the U.S. pilots would train in central Scotland before flying down to South Cerney, England, for the main event.

15

Only a few had to have parts removed to make them fit. By 3:30, everything had been loaded: airplanes, spare parts, tools, luggage.

The team members rode in a very basic passenger compartment, facing backwards, in airline-type seats. Most of them wore earplugs to keep out some of the noise from the C-5's massive engines. There were only two small windows for 75 passengers riding the military transport to England.

The airplanes rode below, in the spacious cargo hold. The passengers not connected with the team who happened to glance down into the hold during the flight were truly amazed to see what looked like an enormous toy shop full of bright little airplanes.

After a nine-hour flight, the C-5 arrived at Royal Air Force Base Mildenhall, a U.S. air base in the east of England, in late afternoon. As the airplanes were unloaded, armed guards kept watch. The pilots, when they taxied their airplanes across the field to a storage hangar, soon saw why. Secret SR-71 Blackbird spy planes, when not in the air, occupied a hangar near theirs. Following a typically English supper of fish and chips (french fries) at the air base hotel, everyone turned in for a much-needed night of sleep.

On Monday morning, when the pilots had recovered from the long flight, it was time to head north to Scotland for the final training session. Soon after breakfast, the pilots took off from Mildenhall. They flew in a loose formation up the east coast of England and then turned toward the west to cross over Edinburgh on their way to Strathallan (STRATH-allen) in central Scotland.

The pilots push their aircraft into the open nose of the C-5.

Debby's plane (above) *is the last to be stowed. The small aerobatic airplanes* (right) *seem like toys in the vast hold of the military transport.*

17

The Strathallan Aerodrome, located in the county of Perthshire, central Scotland, provided a highland retreat for the U.S. competitors.

3
TRAINING IN SCOTLAND

The week of training in Scotland had been a calculated risk, as the weather that far north can make it impossible to fly small planes. Aerobatics needs an area clear of clouds up to at least 3,000 feet (914 meters), as well as good visibility (no rain or mist). But since conditions at the site of the Championships would probably be less than ideal, the team thought that Scotland might provide some very realistic practice. Kermit had arranged for them to stay at Strathallen Aerodrome, where he had once purchased an antique airplane for his own small museum in the United States. The owner of the airfield, Sir William Roberts, had kindly offered space to train, and Kermit had jumped at the chance.

The welcome at Strathallan Aerodrome and Air Museum was in the classic Scottish tradition, and everyone was made to feel at home. The pilots hustled their airplanes into the big hangar where they would share space with World War II airplanes and vintage motorcars.

At Strathallan, the team concentrated heavily on simulated "Unknown" sequences (the third round of competition is called the Unknown round—pilots fly a sequence which they have never practiced in the air before). The team tried to make their practice Unknown flights as much like the third round of Championship flying as possible. Each evening, each pilot received a copy of a

never-before-seen sequence of maneuvers. The pilots could study the required moves during the evening and until they flew before team judges the next morning. But they couldn't practice the moves in the air. That was the way the real Unknown round would work.

The purpose of the Unknown flight is to see how well each pilot can think his or her way through a series of 15 to 17 maneuvers. While each of the individual maneuvers has been practiced in advance, the official arrangement of them has not. It is up to the pilots themselves to work out the problem of matching the exit speed from one maneuver with the entry speed into the next. They must figure out how much altitude will be gained or lost during each maneuver and therefore how high the sequence must be started. And the entire sequence requires a pilot to gauge the effect of winds: how a headwind (blowing from the front), tailwind (from the back), or crosswind (from the side) would affect the airplane's position in the box. Only the most skilled pilots can accurately figure this movement by wind, called **drift**. And the aerobats must even prepare for the rarest of all situations: no wind at all.

For rookies, such mental exercise is intimidating and exhausting. It forces them to realize that aerobatic contests challenge the mind even more than the body. For the experienced competitor, it is an expected part of the game, though it is made more severe by the increased pressures of an international contest.

It is in the Unknown flight that the popular slogan "no zeroes, no outs" best demonstrates a pilot's goal. A "zero" is a maneuver that is disqualified by the judges for being wrongly performed; an "out" is an illegal exit from the strict lines of the box. An individual's ability to fly each maneuver in the right order and within the "box" is worth more than the ability to fly *most* of the maneuvers slightly better than other pilots. Pilots who let the tension get to them and fly maneuvers completely wrong, or who drift beyond the boundaries, are the ones who lose the big chunks of points.

All this was going through the pilots' minds each morning as they finished their coffee and dough rings (doughnuts) in the airfield cafe. The pilots sat in pairs and small groups, pointing out spots on the Unknown sequence diagram which they felt deserved special care. "If you wait too long before pulling the power back for your spin, here, you'll drift so far down the box that you won't have room to do the reverse half Cuban eight. So you may have to force it into the spin....But do it without climbing, or the judges will jump all over you." To the pilots, this made complete sense. To any local Scots who might have

Aerobatics demands physical perfection from the pilot and mechanical perfection from the plane. Here, Debby inspects her Pitts before a routine training flight.

overheard, it was as strange sounding as their Gaelic language was to the Americans.

Debby worked with her long-time friend, the team doctor, Eoin Harvey. Harvey was an aerobatic pilot himself, though not quite of world stature. Debby and Eoin discussed different ways to fly each routine. Debby flew the sequences in her mind and then walked through them out on the airfield. Her left hand held the diagram and her right hand represented her Pitts Special. As she paced back and forth across the little plot of grass, Debby glanced at the sheet of paper and then back to her hand as she twisted and turned it in imitation of the maneuvers her powerful biplane would make.

But such was her concentration that she felt herself flying in great loops and swirls. A brief dip of her right hand toward the ground stood for her plane's long dive at the earth that would rattle the nerves of any but a veteran aerobatic pilot. A quick flip of her wrist meant a **snap roll**, an especially quick and violent roll-over. A simple upward tilt of her flat hand represented a **pull-up**, which would shove her down into the seat of her airplane as if she weighed 650 pounds instead of 110.

Under the guidance of team manager Bob Carmichael, an airline captain and former competitor, the team turned its

The "humpty-bump"

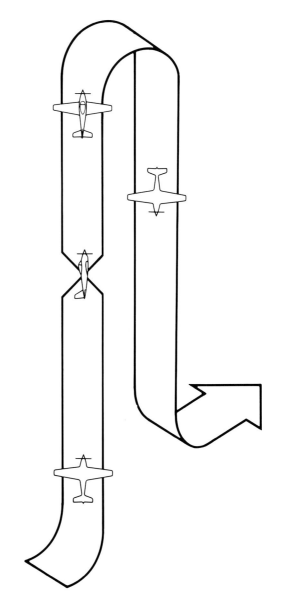

attention to the choice of a maneuver for the official Unknown flight. At the Championships, each country would contribute one maneuver, and then the International Jury would combine them into a flyable **sequence**. The general idea was to pick a move that the U.S. pilots liked to fly, but one which their main rivals might find especially difficult. Then the American pilots would practice that maneuver until it had become second nature.

The maneuver they agreed upon went by a name meaningful only to themselves: "outside push-push-push **humpty-bump** with a snap up." The American maneuver for the Unknown sequence really boiled down to a snap roll flown straight up, which did not go all the way around to where it began. Starting the maneuver upside down added to its difficulty by restricting the pilot's view of what was happening.

There was a lot more to the final training session than just the fine points of Unknown flights. After each morning contest, the pilots used their practice time to fly through the Known sequence. The Known sequence had been published before the start of the season and was flown in every contest in every country during the year. Also, the whole team ran through their Freestyle flights. The Freestyle is the last round in competition.

The wifferdill

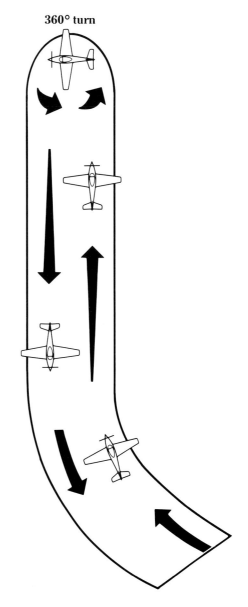

360° turn

Each pilot designs his or her own Freestyle program, filled with their favorite maneuvers, which the judges grade mostly on creative merit. Debby, for instance, spent a lot of time working on a new maneuver called a "wifferdill." It consisted of flying straight up until the airplane ran out of speed and began to tip over on one wing. In the common maneuver called a **hammerhead**, the airplane rotates until its nose is pointing down and then dives back downward for a few seconds. But in a "wifferdill," the plane continues to rotate until the nose is pointing back up at the sky and then continues around. Or, at least it is supposed to point back up.

Only chief mechanic Ray Williams had been able to get a Pitts Special to do this maneuver. Ray managed to work it out in his own Pitts, but only after a lot of special adjustments to the wings. Debby worked at her "wifferdill" time after time after time. She was able to get as far as three-quarters of the way around, but no more before the plane's nose started to fall toward the ground. Determined to conquer this unusual maneuver and use it in her Four-Minute flight, she kept at it. But the lack of special adjustments, and probably the difference in her plane's balance caused by her weighing only half as much as Ray, finally forced her to realize that "wifferdills" were too risky to try in the Championships. Failure there would be measured in points, not just in her teammates' wisecracks.

Despite concerns over the likelihood of bad weather in central Scotland, the Americans were able to practice intensively nearly every day. At this stage, the team was about as ready as it could have been. Debby saw the team's readiness in this way: "I think Strathallan was an excellent session. We had a wind to contend with, and the box was absolutely the most difficult one I have ever flown in. It didn't line up with anything, there was nothing on the horizon that was a clue to where you were. You *had* to notice the markers on the ground. It felt like we were probably stronger than we had been. I think we all had a lot of confidence, and I don't think it was unjustified."

4

SOUTH TO ENGLAND

But the main event of the long, expensive trip was in England, not Scotland. And so on Friday, August 1, everything and everyone was packed up for another move—450 miles (725 kilometers) south to Gloucestershire (GLOSS-ter-shur). The airplanes again headed out in formation while the rest of the crew and supporters piled into vans and rental cars.

The trip south started out in perfect weather. Some of Debby's teammates felt that the journey should be used for more flying practice. But, as they flew closer to England, the weather turned grayer, and the view from the air became less scenic and more industrial. There was no more talk of training. The real competition was quickly approaching.

The pilots headed down England's west coast, stopping briefly at Blackpool to refuel and stretch their legs. When they breezed into South Cerney (SIR-nee), they were greeted by an almost-empty airfield. The crowd of airplanes they had expected had been slowed down by poor weather in several directions. But each country's planes would get there, somehow.

The airfield was a true aerodrome, a large area of reasonably smooth grass without any marked runways. If the wind was from the east, you took off and landed to the east; if it was from the southwest, you took off and landed to the southwest. A large arrow on the ground could be moved by hand to point

into the wind so arriving pilots could tell which way to land. In addition, a cloth sleeve, or windsock, flew from a pole to show the wind direction.

South Cerney's old control tower and administration building had been taken over by the Championship organizers. Directly in front of these buildings was a large grass plot surrounded by small tents and temporary buildings. These shelters would serve as individual headquarters for the teams. A large mess tent, where everyone would eat during the competition, stood to one side. Beyond the mess tent were the parking areas for the aerobatic airplanes. These were arranged by country and included plenty of space between rows for easy taxiing.

After registering, the Americans climbed into their ground vehicles,

Kermit completes his preparations by topping off his oil tank.

including a van provided by Championships-sponsor Volkswagen, and drove to nearby Cirencester (SI-ren-sess-ter) and the Royal College of Agriculture, which would be their home for more than two weeks. A group of solid stone buildings, the College looked like a castle on the outside and like an older college dormitory on the inside. The rooms were simple, basic, and barely large enough for two.

Back at South Cerney, aerobatics was everywhere and spreading. Teams seemed to appear out of nowhere: the Czechs with their fine, factory-built **Zlin monoplanes**; the West Germans with a mixture of Czech Zlins, American Pitts, and their own new **Extra 230**; then came the Italians with mainly French airplanes, and the Spanish with Zlins. Along with the pilots came mechanics and judges and interpreters and team captains and delegates to important committees and, of course, the most dedicated fans.

Soon, the only ones who hadn't made an appearance were the Soviets. Rumor had it that they had arrived by military transport at the Bristol airport not far away. The pilots already at South Cerney didn't know exactly which airplanes the Russians would be flying, as the Soviet entry forms didn't agree with the rumors coming back from Bristol. At last, toward the end of the final day for arrivals, three sleek airplanes with red stars on their tails buzzed low over the field in close formation. The Russians had arrived!

They landed and were immediately surrounded by a mini-United Nations. Everyone from every country tried to get a close look. At first, the Soviet's new planes seemed to be the same **Sukhoi** (SOO-koy) 26s that hadn't been very impressive in 1984. Little by little, the true story dribbled out: the airplanes looked familiar, but they were packed full of expensive new ideas. Exotic materials like **carbon fiber** and **titanium**, which had always been used only in airliners and military planes, made these planes stronger and faster. Because of the expense and the secrecy connected with the new designs, the planes were government-owned and would be shared by all the Russian pilots.

The other teams could console themselves with the knowledge that aerobatics depends more on pilots than airplanes. The Soviets' new planes might be able to climb like a rocket and spin like a top, but the contest would be won by the most talented and experienced pilot.

The revolutionary Soviet Sukhoi Su-26M waits in the sun at South Cerney.

French pilot Louis Pena races the engine of his sleek Capena.

A Hungarian pilot runs a last minute check on his Zlin 50.

Long hours of practice could equal the benefit of new materials and design.

The judges also concerned the Americans. Like judges who score sports such as figure skating and diving, aerobatic judges sit in a row and call out scores from 0 to 10. Some judges have gone through a formal training program and have come up through the ranks from local contests to the international level. Many have judged in 50 or more events. But some of the judges from smaller countries like Romania and Spain have gained far less experience, since their countries have fewer contests each year than some American states. Such judges may not be up to the challenge of scoring more than 200 flights of 15-20 maneuvers each.

The pilots knew, then, that there was a chance that the judging might be uneven in quality. But people who let themselves get discouraged easily usually don't get as far as their national team, and Rihn and Weeks and the rest had faced obstacles before and conquered them. No matter how great the Soviet Sukhois looked, their pilots would have to fly them better in order to score more points. The next few days would reveal if they were up to that task.

Before long, it was time for practice "in the box." Each pilot was scheduled for 20 minutes of practice flying within the invisible boundaries of air above the contest site. Debby and her teammates were more concerned with getting to know the territory than with rehearsing maneuvers. Aerobatics is a sport of lightning decisions based on a pilot's solid knowledge of landmarks: a church steeple, a factory's smokestack, a group of farm buildings. Any hesitation in lining up the plane with a landmark would be detected by the judges. A major error could throw the remainder of a flight out of rhythm and its pilot out of the running.

As each hour passed, the pressure increased. Since leaving Scotland, the pilots had gone four days without practice. Normally, that would be no great problem. But in world-class aerobatics, any lay-off hurts. A pilot's timing will be off, his or her reflexes won't be quite what they should be, and the pain of g-forces will seem more severe even if it really isn't. So the Americans welcomed the start of practice. Walter Egger, a popular Austrian pilot, took off at 10:15 on the morning of Sunday, August 3, for his trial flight in the box. By the time he landed, 20 minutes later, visibility was worsening and the rain was getting heavy. Egger was the first and last to practice on opening day.

Gloom settled in as the rain came down harder. The formal opening ceremonies, during which the aerobatic teams march in uniform behind their flags as in the Olympics, were moved into a large hangar. There was no marching, just a lot of people standing around trying not to look uncomfortable. The manager of the West German team wore a life jacket over his team blazer in an attempt to cut some of the tension.

By the time all of the distinguished guests and officials had spoken and the Championships had been officially opened, the rain had stopped and the skies were clearing, just the way the meteorologist had predicted. But it was too late to do any more flying, and so everyone had a traditional English afternoon tea with cakes and drifted back to the College.

The next day was better, with skies alternately clear and overcast, and a few pilots practiced. Tuesday was better yet, and the pilots flew a full day of practice, but the Championships were already a full day behind schedule. Wednesday dawned clear but then began to cloud over as the wind picked up.

That Wednesday, the world got its first good look at the much-improved Soviet Sukhoi 26M. The airplane looked like it had the power and control to do anything its pilot commanded it to do. It could climb almost forever, drawing the most dramatic lines in the sky. But as it climbed, the wind blew it farther and farther off course, sometimes right out of the box. Impressive as it was, the Sukhoi wasn't perfect. Debby saw it this way: "I wasn't impressed [by the Soviet women pilots] . . . I was impressed by their airplane. A couple of them really pushed the airplane hard, but I didn't think they looked that strong. The maneuvers were not well executed, the wind carried them away. They couldn't stay in the box. It was as if the airplane and the wind were just ahead of them."

Briefings, like the one pictured above, are an essential part of any international competition. But at South Cerney, the meetings were especially important. The pilots would find out during the morning meetings if the day's flying had been cancelled due to bad weather.

5
THE CHAMPIONSHIPS BEGIN

Thursday, August 7, dawned cloudy and windy, gradually improving enough to permit the pilots to finish practice. But it had taken five days for 70 practice flights and now the Championships were two days behind schedule. If the weather cooperated, two lost days would be no problem. The Championships' schedule included some extra days. In the evening, back at the College, pilots drew lots for starting positions for the first and second rounds of flying. At last, it looked like the actual contest was about to get underway.

The next morning, there was an eight o'clock briefing. James Black, a veteran English pilot, presided. He greeted the 100 or more men and women crowded into the briefing tent and then introduced the main contest officials, who would become familiar during the next two weeks. Then Black asked the meteorologist to predict the flying conditions, always a tense time. On Friday, August 8, the forecast was "low ceilings which will tend to lift as the temperature rises." No one realized it at the time, but the meteorologist could have taped his speech and replayed it almost every morning.

The clouds finally rose to about 3,000 feet (914 meters) by 10:30, and the first flight was in the air a few minutes later. This began the first round—the Known-Compulsory flight—a series of maneuvers which had been published at the beginning of the year and which was by now familiar to everyone.

First to fly was French pilot Claude Bessiere, who amazed everyone with a truly excellent flight despite the added pressure of being first and thus unable to watch anyone else fly the sequence. Debby Rihn was the first American to fly. Because of Debby's great rookie year, the other competitors expected much of her. Her fine practice sessions seemed to point to an even better second Championships.

Off she went in her red, white, and blue Pitts Special, its 200-horsepower (149.2-kilowatt) engine pulling her up to several thousand feet in just over a minute. She rocked her wings as a signal to the judges that she was ready to begin and charged into the opening maneuver: 1½ rolls straight up. She quickly finished that maneuver flying upside down and slowed for her entry into the 1½-turn inverted spin. For four minutes she flitted from one end of the 1,000-meter box to the other, using snap rolls, tailslides, rolling turns, hammerheads, and hesitation rolls.

Debby flew each maneuver as required...but not exactly as she had practiced. The pressure of competition had affected her performance slightly. There were little bobbles here and there, and hesitation where there should have been smoothness. It just didn't look like the Debby who had zipped through dozens of training flights with few errors. But this wasn't training: it was the real thing. And while there had been little pressure on her in her first World Championships, since no one expected anything of a rookie, she now had a reputation to live up to. It was a different game.

After her last maneuver—a vertical snap roll—Debby rocked her wings signifying the end of the flight and pulled out of the box. As the next pilot was taking off, she slowed, descended, and landed on the smooth grass. She taxied over to her parking place, and the glum look on her face made it clear she knew the flight had not been up to her ability. She sat in the cockpit going over the flight, maneuver by maneuver, trying to figure out what had gone wrong. Team members came up to her and offered words of encouragement, but she knew she had not flown the way she was capable of flying.

"I didn't feel like it was a really bad flight," she reflected afterwards. "I wasn't happy with being the seventh to fly. The judges need to warm up, they aren't necessarily going to score the first few flights well. I really don't know what went wrong...I felt like it wasn't my strongest flight. I wasn't pleased with it, but there was nothing dramatically wrong with it."

Debby's problems notwithstanding, the contest went on. The weather held and the flying order went smoothly. By

This shot of South Cerney shows the team headquarters at left (striped tents), *the dining hall at right* (white tent), *and the administration building in the center.*

4:00 P.M., half of the 70 pilots had flown. And by the end of the day—7:30 P.M.—all but nine pilots had gotten through their first flights. The contest was now moving along quickly after the discouraging delays of practice. Morale was high as everyone gathered back at the College for an outdoor barbecue.

The next morning, it was the same story as the first day: low clouds. The teams trooped out of the briefing tent, took a long look at the sky, and then headed to the mess tent for coffee, tea, and grumbling. They had come to fly, not to stare at the sky! But every few minutes, someone poked his head outside to do just that—stare upwards.

It seemed to be getting lighter, and the clouds looked a little higher. But improvement came slowly, and the first flight didn't get off the ground until 11:00 A.M.

It was just after noon when the 70th flight of the first round finished. One of the last to fly was Kermit Weeks, who roared through his 16 maneuvers with the supreme confidence of years of World Championship flying. His sleek, black *Solution* was equal to every challenge.

Then the computer went to work on the scores: multiplying, adding, and then analyzing. Pilots and crews alike came running when the unofficial scores were posted. Among the men, Soviet pilots Nikitiuk and Smolin had taken a strong lead, followed closely by the reigning champion, Jirmus of Czechoslovakia. Kermit placed fourth out of 56 men and helped give his team a solid hold on second place. The women did well, despite Debby's disappointing eighth place. Her teammates Julie Pfile and Linda Meyers placed high enough to put the Americans in second, just like the men, behind the Soviet team. It was a good start, and there was plenty of time to climb to the top.

Kermit, right, and Henry Haigh, a veteran competitor, watch Debby's first flight.

6
THE SECOND SEQUENCE

The second round of flying was the "Freestyle." Each pilot had designed his or her own sequence to fit a set of rules which guarantees the sequences will be equal in overall difficulty. There can be no more than 20 maneuvers, and there must be at least one of every basic type of aerobatic figure: figure-eight, tailslide, inside and outside spin, inside and outside snap roll, etc. Like the Known flight, this one could be practiced just as much as each pilot wanted. And most of the aerobats had flown their Freestyle sequences dozens of times.

The second round began midway through Saturday afternoon. After the judges posted the first round scores, the competition stopped for two hours so that protests could be filed. (In world-class competition, protests are filed almost routinely, over any number of issues—such as one pilot being forced to fly in a stronger wind than another.) Twenty-two pilots flew before it got dark,

including Americans Patty Wagstaff and Linda Meyers. Patty, the only rookie on the U.S. team, flew very well and caught on quickly to the novel atmosphere of a World Championships. Linda, however, let the pressure get to her, and she zeroed two of the 20 maneuvers.

The contest was almost back on schedule, but Sunday took care of that! It rained all morning, stopped briefly at 2:30 to permit four pilots to fly, and then started up again. Along with the rain came worsening visibility.

Monday was another gray day. The rain had stopped, but the clouds were much too low for safe aerobatics. At 4:30, the officials faced reality and called the day's flights off. Tuesday wasn't much better. One of the French women took off, climbed up, decided she couldn't see anything, and landed. The day's flying was cancelled at 5:00 P.M., at which time the clouds began to break up! But it was too late to get things reorganized.

In 3½ days, the judges were able to score just 25 flights out of the required 70 for the second round. People were starting to worry. The contest was scheduled to end in three more days, and there were 115 flights still to be flown. The international rules say that if three full rounds aren't completed, the Championships will not be officially recognized. Any thought of making it all the way to the fourth round had long since been abandoned. Though 28 pilots flew on Wednesday, there was talk of having to scratch the World Aerobatics Championships for the first time in history.

The prospect of two years of hard work coming to nothing was too upsetting to consider. Losing would be better than having no decision at all.

But time was running short, and unless the weather suddenly changed completely, the unthinkable could happen. People were starting to count the hours remaining and to calculate how many flights could be completed if...

One of Wednesday's flights was Debby Rihn's, and it was a good one. "I don't know if I flew better for having to concentrate more... it had been quite a few days [since my last flight]. The weather was not great; in fact, one flight after I flew, they shut down the contest.

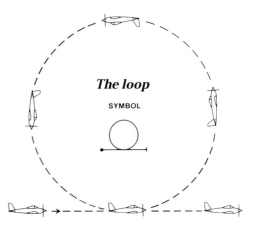

The symbols shown above and to the right — called Aresti symbols — are part of an international aerobatic code.

There were some scattered low clouds, very, very poor visibility, and they had changed the direction of the box [because the wind had shifted]. I know I was flying more aggressively...I was really driving my lines down and had a lot of speed."

On Thursday, the next-to-last scheduled day of flying, the clouds didn't rise above the minimum height until 3:00 P.M. Judges raced out to their posts, and the first airplane was in the air in a few minutes. By quitting time, 18 more pilots were able to fly, including Kermit Weeks, who had another excellent flight.

There were now just 10 pilots who hadn't completed their second flights. Only one day remained for these ten to fly the second round and for all of the pilots to fly the third round. Teams from every country were showing signs of tension, as time was running out with so much yet to do.

Wind was the problem on Friday, along with international red tape. One of the big problems at any World Championships is getting all the countries to agree on even the slightest change in the rules. Each delegation assumes that a change is being made to give one country an unfair advantage over the others. This suspicion leads to long discussions and arguments and meetings of committees and teams.

Not until 6:00 P.M. did the winds slacken enough, and the clouds rise enough, for flying to be resumed. By then, the situation seemed hopeless because the next day, Saturday, had been set aside for the World Festival of Aerobatics. The Festival was to be a spectacular, day-long airshow and had been advertised around the country as something the whole family could enjoy and appreciate.

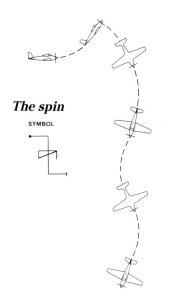

The spin

SYMBOL

But among the pilots there was no thought of quitting. The last four competitors flew their Freestyle programs, including American Julie Pfile, who had her second excellent flight. Then, without a pause, the third program began—the Unknown round. The International Jury had composed the required routine in secret during the contest, and none of the pilots would be allowed to practice it in the air. Their first try at it would be in full view of the judges.

By international rule, there was supposed to be a two-hour wait between the end of one round and the start of the next, for protests to be filed and considered. But there was no time to waste. The two-hour period was observed, but third-round flying began at the same time. Several teams had talked about filing protests because some of the pilots had been forced to fly in winds that probably were above the legal limits. But everyone now agreed that it was more important to try to complete the Championships.

The results of the second round were posted while the flying continued. No one filed a protest and the standings became official. They showed that Kermit Weeks had captured the silver medal in the men's division, and Clint McHenry had won the bronze. The added points boosted Kermit into second place, overall, and Clint into third. Their scores so far, plus Henry Haigh's, put the U.S. men into a good lead for the Nesterov Trophy, which they had won in 1984.

In the women's competition, Debby Rihn won the bronze medal for her second flight and moved all the way up from eighth to third in the overall standings. Julie Pfile slipped one notch overall to fourth, while rookie Patty Wagstaff moved up from tenth to sixth. Despite the confusion over the fate of the contest, spirits in the American camp were high.

The slow roll

SYMBOL

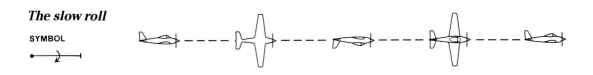

7

THE FINAL ROUND

Friday's flying ended with 66 pilots still to complete the third round. Faced with a desperate situation, the contest organizers agreed to continue the flying in and around the World Festival of Aerobatics. It would have been just too heartbreaking for everyone involved to admit defeat.

Bright and early on Saturday, everyone filed in for the morning briefing. The situation was hopeful: if everything worked out exactly as planned, there might actually be enough time to finish the contest. If *everything* worked! If there wasn't a single delay for weather. If no one filed a protest. And if the judges did not decide to take an hour for lunch. It was a long shot, to be sure. But it was possible that the 1986 World Championships might yet see champions crowned.

The only thing left to do was fly and fly and fly. And maybe if there were just a few pilots left when it got too dark to fly, they might voluntarily withdraw. As

soon as the short briefing was over, everyone charged into action. The first pilot was in the air in a matter of minutes, and, as soon as he landed, another was on the way. All morning and right through lunch hour they flew (there would be plenty of time to eat when the contest was over).

By late morning, the airshow crowd was pouring through the gates by the thousands. The weather, for once, cooperated. The scene was very much like a country fair, with rides to keep

The West German team races the clock to repair one of the Zlin 50s. Repairs go on throughout the competition, and teams often exchange tools and expertise.

the youngest children busy while their parents enjoyed the exhibition of international aviation. It was a grand excuse for a Sunday outing and picnic, and a true drama was unfolding above the spectators: the Thirteenth World Aerobatics Championships was struggling to complete its task.

Debby Rihn took one last look at the diagram of the Unknown flight. She had gotten her copy more than a week ago, and while it was now as familiar as the instrument panel of her faithful Pitts Special, there couldn't be any harm in checking it once more. There might be some little clue that would help her get a bit more performance out of her airplane.

Debby had spent what seemed like hours walking back and forth over a small square of grass, "flying" the series of maneuvers with her hand. With total concentration, Debby willed her hand straight up and felt she was flying straight up. Her hand/airplane pivoted downward, and she dove toward the ground, seeing not the grass a few feet away but the aerobatic box rushing up at almost 200 mph (322 kph).

This is the only way to practice the Unknown flight, the only way to memorize every motion of each of the 17 maneuvers. Debby's hand neared the pretend "edge of the box," and she smoothly spun around, imagining the boundary judges who would soon be lining her up through their sighting wires. She dove, she climbed, she rolled and spun. To someone who happened to walk by, she might have looked like a person practicing some strange kind of dance. Chances are that she would never have noticed the puzzled observer, so intent was she on maneuvers and the box and the imaginary wind.

Finally, it was time for Debby to fly. It was time to find out if all the pretend flying in the pretend aerobatic box had prepared her for the real thing. She climbed into her small biplane, hooked up the straps of her shoulder harness, two lap belts, and parachute. Then she pulled extra hard on each one so that even when she was experiencing five or six times the force of gravity, the belts would remain tight.

One of the mechanics swung her propeller. Her engine coughed a few times and then caught on and picked up speed. She let it warm up, and, when the temperature and pressure gauges said it was ready, she released the brakes and began to taxi out to the end of the grass takeoff area. She glanced up to see World Champion Petr Jirmus finish his Unknown flight, and then she got the signal to take off. She pushed on the throttle, the engine roared, and off she went, bouncing a few times and then rising into the air.

Above: Debby (seated left), *along with Julie Pfile* (standing) *and team doctor Eoin Harvey* (right), *concentrate on the afternoon's flying. Below: Debby prepares mentally for her own flight.*

The Pitts, with its nose pointed upward, climbed like only a light, powerful airplane can. In barely a minute, Debby was at her starting altitude, ready to roll upside down during her dive to gain speed for the start. She rocked her wings three times, to let the judges know she was about to begin, and then pushed hard on the control stick. The blood rushed to her head as the airplane pushed around to head straight up. Just as it became fully vertical, she pushed a rudder pedal and then quickly reversed the controls to stop the roll as the airplane got halfway around. She then pushed the stick forward again and briefly flew level and upright to end the first maneuver.

Back and forth across the 1,000-meter box she sped, flipping and turning in the most intricate way. One after another, she tackled the difficult maneuvers. Her movements were precise and in the right order. Then came maneuver 16, when everything seemed to come apart. Instead of rolling all the way around, Debby rolled just ¾ of the way, which sent her flying off 90° in the wrong direction.

"I was concentrating so much on keeping it in the box and doing things slower [to reduce the effect of the high wind] that I really wasn't aware of going slower. When I pushed up, I had kind of let my guard down. It was the second-

While climbing at top speed, nose pointed straight in the air, a pilot can become dizzy from the "increased" force of gravity.

to-the-last maneuver, and I felt that I had made it through the most difficult part of the sequence. This maneuver and the last were maneuvers I had in my Freestyle, that I did day after day, and I guess I relaxed a little too soon.

45

"I pushed up and instead of really looking out to see where I was, I pushed up at a slower speed and did my vertical roll primarily on timing, and not as much on making sure I had done 360° of rotation. I only rolled ¾ instead of a full roll and I didn't catch it. I was concerned with getting blown out of the box, and I stopped it just perfect. I was in the box and I was really pleased for that, and I went on and completed the maneuver.

"When I pulled out of the maneuver, I realized I was going the wrong way! At that point, I was very upset with myself...it was nobody's fault but my own. I then made a 90° turn [to get back on course], pulled up and did the last maneuver." Debby was crushed. The momentary lapse cost her about 300 points for having zeroed maneuver 16 and another 150 points for the unscheduled 90° turn. Together, the loss of 450 points dropped her from third place—and a bronze medal on the Unknown flight—down to tenth place. For the overall contest, the error dropped her from fourth place to sixth. Knowing how expensive any slip will be is what works to create the tremendous pressure of a World Championships.

The next to fly was American Harold Chappell, a relaxed, experienced pilot who pulled off his best Championships flight yet. Then it was time for Kermit to fly. He was in second place, only 130 points out of the lead. His airplane was running at top form and he was ready. After the same warm-up ritual Debby had gone through, he taxied out and took off. His big engine lifted him to starting altitude, and soon he was roaring into the box to begin a rapid series of maneuvers.

Kermit's flight was clearly one of the best. He was followed by the next pilot in line, and the next and the next. By 2:00 P.M., 40 of the 70 pilots had flown. If the weather held, there was a chance that all the flights could be completed before sunset. But an air display had to be staged for the thousands of people who had driven and cycled from all over England to see it.

While hundreds of aerobatic pilots and team members paced back and forth, the air display got underway. First to take the air was the pride of British (and French) aviation, the Concorde supersonic airliner, flown by Mike Riley. Riley, a British Airways captain, was a pilot on the 1976 British Aerobatic Team.

Kermit climbs in the Solution *to begin his sequence.*

The Concorde is a supersonic (faster than sound) aircraft. Originally built in a joint effort between Britain and France, the Concorde was first used commercially in the mid-1970s. Its distinctive nose has become associated the world over with speed and fine technical design.

Gleaming white, the Concorde brought cheers from the crowd. Next came a pair of 40-year-old fighter planes—a Spitfire and a Hurricane—from the Battle of Britain, one of the turning points of World War II. They swooped low across the field while old-timers explained to their grandchildren how these planes helped to win the war.

The newly-named Soviet "Red Stars" team gave its first performance in the West. The three Soviet Sukhoi aerobatic planes made several spirited fly-bys, showing off the power and maneuverability of the new machine. This was followed by a full performance of the Royal Air Force's "Red Arrows" nine-plane jet team, flying bright red Hawk trainers. In perfect formation, they swooped and looped and then changed formation, all the while trailing spectacular combinations of red, white, and blue smoke.

One by one, in and around the air display, the contestants got to fly. By 4:00 P.M., when the formal display ended, there were 23 pilots left to fly. Then the most intense part of the drama began. Each of the remaining pilots had barely nine minutes to take off, climb, fly the sequence, and land, before official sunset at 7:30. Any interruption would ruin the chance of an official World Championships. The weather would have to remain above the minimums required for the cloud ceiling, visibility, and wind (or everyone, including the officials, would have to pretend it was).

Kermit "walks through" his flight plan with his hand as model.

Britain's Royal Air Force Red Arrows perform a complex routine.

Waiting for a break in the air show schedule, pilot Linda Meyers discusses wind conditions with Kermit.

One by one, the pilots took off and flew without wasting a minute. Every member of every team cooperated, because everyone's goal was now the same: to finish the contest before nightfall. Little by little, the sun was getting lower and dimmer. Even though this was the middle of August, it was chilly and getting cold, but hardly anyone left. Spectators just pulled their collars up, stuffed their hands in their pockets, and shivered.

Soon it was 7:00 P.M. There were only four pilots who hadn't flown. As each one finished, 100 people silently calculated the time needed to finish: if these last four average just 7½ minutes, we can do it. But if they take eight minutes or more, then the last flight will have to be scrubbed. The thought of ending the Championships with one pilot waiting to fly was too painful to consider. The pilots and organizers were too close to give up now.

Finally the last pilot, Brigitte DeLasalle-Lesage of France, climbed into her plane. She took off, flew her sequence in the dim light, and rocked the wings of her low-wing DL 260 to signal the end of her flight and of the Thirteenth World Championships—with only four minutes left before sunset.

Later that night, an official walked into the College hall with the first copy of the scores for the third round and posted it near the door. A crowd of people pushed close to see. There were surprises and, for the American team, disappointments. While Americans Linda Meyers and Julie Pfile had taken gold and silver medals in the last round, Soviet pilots had taken the top two places among the men.

As soon as the startling numbers appeared, out came the notepads and hand calculators. Would the U.S. men's 350-point lead hold up despite the high scores for the Soviets and the disappointing flights of McHenry and Haigh? The numbers were added and then added again. Each time the calculators told the same crushing story: the U.S. had lost the Nesterov Trophy by 37½ points, out of a possible 40,000 points!

Fortunately, there was good news. Julie Pfile's silver medal performance in the third round lifted her from fourth place to second in the final standings. One of the pilots she passed, unfortunately, was teammate Debby Rihn. But Julie's medal marked three straight years that the U.S. women had held on to second place against tough odds.

The mood of the U.S. team was an unsettled mixture of joy and defeat. The two hours of waiting for the scores to be made official weren't the most enjoyable of the whole trip, by a long shot. Americans would take home a lot of medals, but the important trophies would stay in Europe.

At last, around midnight, the formalities began. The closing ceremonies were not held in front of tens of thousands of spectators at the air display, but in a small, intimate hall. Aerobatics officials presented trophies and medals and spoke the appropriate words of praise. The pilots, whose day had begun 18 hours before, were exhausted.

Suddenly, it was all over. The day had started with almost no hope of success. But each team had helped and sacrificed to make the most of each moment.

Debby and her teammates began immediately to look toward 1988 and the Championships in Red Deer, Alberta, Canada. For the long hours in the C-5 on the way home, they discussed new ways to master their planes and to bring the Nesterov Trophy home again. Victories and defeats are temporary, while the sport of aerobatics goes on as long as there are pilots like Debby Rihn and Kermit Weeks willing to devote an important part of their lives to flying perfect loops and rolls and spins.

Although the aerobatics awards ceremonies bring the American pilots no money or real fame, they are times of immense national and personal pride.

Again, the C-5 accepts all of the tiny aerobatic planes—this time for the long ride home to the United States.

APPENDIX

FIRST ROUND
WOMEN'S INDIVIDUAL STANDINGS

1. Lubova Nemkova	USSR	Sukhoi Su-26M	3,780.0
2. Irina Adabash	USSR	Sukhoi Su-26M	3,763.2
3. Julie Pfile	USA	Pitts Special	3,737.2
4. Chalide Makagonova	USSR	Sukhoi Su-26M	3,726.9
5. Catherine Manoury	France	TR 260	3,720.4

MEN'S INDIVIDUAL STANDINGS

1. Nikolai Nikitiuk	USSR	Sukhoi Su-26M	4,088.1
2. Victor Smolin	USSR	Sukhoi Su-26M	4,082.8
3. Petr Jirmus	Czechoslovakia	Zlin 50LS	4,066.3
4. Kermit Weeks	USA	Weeks Solution	3,993.2
5. Henry Haigh	USA	Haigh Super Star	3,982.0

WOMEN'S TEAM

1. USSR	11,270.1
2. USA	11,134.4
3. France	10,848.8

MEN'S TEAM

1. USSR	12,124.5
2. USA	11,939.4
3. Czechoslovakia	11,783.0

SECOND ROUND
WOMEN'S INDIVIDUAL STANDINGS

1. Lubova Nemkova	USSR	Sukhoi Su-26M	5,927.4
2. Catherine Manoury	France	TR 260	5,778.9
3. Debby Rihn	USA	Pitts Special	5,675.4
4. Patty Wagstaff	USA	Pitts Special	5,628.8
5. Julie Pfile	USA	Pitts Special	5,552.3

MEN'S INDIVIDUAL STANDINGS

1. Petr Jirmus	Czechoslovakia	Zlin 50LS	6,173.9
2. Kermit Weeks	USA	Weeks Solution	6,117.4
3. Clint McHenry	USA	Extra 230	6,042.8
4. Patrick Paris	France	CAP 230	6,021.6
5. Louis Pena	France	Capena	5,963.0

AFTER TWO ROUNDS
WOMEN'S INDIVIDUAL STANDINGS

1. Lubova Nemkova	USSR	Sukhoi Su-26M	9,707.4
2. Catherine Manoury	France	TR 260	9,499.3
3. Debby Rihn	USA	Pitts Special	9,353.4
4. Julie Pfile	USA	Pitts Special	9,289.5
5. Irina Adabash	USSR	Sukhoi Su-26M	9,235.8

MEN'S INDIVIDUAL STANDINGS

1. Petr Jirmus	Czechoslovakia	Zlin 50LS	10,240.2
2. Kermit Weeks	USA	Week's Solution	10,110.6
3. Clint McHenry	USA	Extra 230	10,007.1
4. Nikolai Nikitiuk	USSR	Sukhoi Su-26M	9,969.8
5. Patrick Paris	France	CAP 230	9,937.5

WOMEN'S TEAM

1. USSR	28,113.3
2. USA	27,847.4
3. France	27,045.8

MEN'S TEAM

1. USA	30,046.1
2. USSR	29,699.4
3. France	29,360.5

THIRD ROUND
WOMEN'S INDIVIDUAL STANDINGS

1. Linda Meyers	USA	Abernathy Streaker	3,405.5
2. Julie Pfile	USA	Pitts Special	3,386.3
3. Lubova Nemkova	USSR	Sukhoi Su-26M	3,262.2
4. Irina Adabash	USSR	Sukhoi Su-26M	3,123.2
5. Catherine Manoury	France	TR 260	3,076.4

MEN'S INDIVIDUAL STANDINGS

1. Victor Smolin	USSR	Sukhoi Su-26M	3,622.5
2. Nikolai Nikitiuk	USSR	Sukhoi Su-26M	3,570.1
3. Kermit Weeks	USA	Weeks Solution	3,565.6
4. Petr Jirmus	Czechoslovakia	Zlin 50LS	3,557.4
5. Eric Muller	Switzerland	Extra 230	2,525.4

FINAL RESULTS
WOMEN'S INDIVIDUAL CHAMPIONSHIP

1. Lubova Nemkova	USSR	Sukhoi Su-26M	12,969.6
2. Julie Pfile	USA	Pitts Special	12,675.8
3. Catherine Manoury	France	TR 260	12,575.7
4. Irina Adabash	USSR	Sukhoi Su-26M	12,359.0
5. Chalide Makagonova	USSR	Sukhoi Su-26M	12,175.2
6. Debby Rihn	USA	Pitts Special	12,060.5

MEN'S INDIVIDUAL CHAMPIONSHIP

1. Petr Jirmus	Czechoslovakia	Zlin 50LS	13,797.6
2. Kermit Weeks	USA	Weeks Solution	13,676.1
3. Victor Smolin	USSR	Sukhoi Su-26M	13,547.1
4. Nikolai Nikitiuk	USSR	Sukhoi Su-26M	13,540.0
5. Christian Schweizer	Switzerland	Extra 230	13,414.0

WOMEN'S TEAM CHAMPIONSHIP

1. USSR	37,503.8
2. USA	36,690.3
3. France	35,475.6

MEN'S TEAM CHAMPIONSHIP

1. USSR	40,297.2
2. USA	40,259.8
3. France	39,312.7

GLOSSARY

aileron—the movable control surfaces near the tips of the wings which make the airplane roll from side to side

aerobatic box—the invisible block of air above the airfield where all maneuvers must be performed. It is 1,000 meters (3,281 feet) wide, 1,000 meters deep, and 1,000 meters high, and has its bottom 100 meters (328 feet) above the ground.

biplane—an airplane with two wings, one above the other

carbon fiber—a high-tech material made from thin strands of carbon. It is unusually strong and light.

drift—an airplane's unwanted movement caused by a wind

elevator—the movable control surface at the rear of the horizontal part of the tail which makes the nose of the airplane point up or down

Extra 230—a West German aerobatic monoplane based on the American Laser design

Four-Minute sequence—the fourth stage in an aerobatic contest, in which the emphasis is on the overall artistic impression, rather than on precision

Freestyle sequence—the second stage in an aerobatic contest in which the maneuvers are chosen by each pilot

g-forces—the pressure exerted on pilot and airplane by sharp maneuvering. This force is measured in multiples of the pull of gravity.

groundcrew—all the members of a team except the pilots: mechanics, trainer, judge, doctor, interpreter

half Cuban eight—a maneuver consisting of half a figure eight in which the airplane rolls back upright before finishing

hammerhead—a maneuver in which the airplane flies straight up, pivots on a wing, and dives straight back down

humpty-bump—a maneuver in which the airplane flies straight up, does a roll, and then arcs back down again

inside—that portion of any maneuver flown with the pilot's head toward the inside of a circle or loop

Known sequence—the first stage in an aerobatic contest, in which all pilots fly the same series of maneuvers

loop—a vertical circle in the sky which looks like the letter "O"

maneuver—any shape drawn in the sky by an airplane which starts and ends with the airplane flying level

minimums—the limits on the cloud level, wind speed, and visibility for a contest to be held with safety

monoplane—an airplane with one wing, half of which is on either side of the cockpit

outside—that portion of any maneuver flown with the pilot's head toward the outside of a circle or loop

Pitts Special—an American aerobatic biplane used in contest flying for 40 years

pull-up—making an airplane's nose point up by pulling on its control stick. This produces g-forces.

roll—to move the ailerons so that the airplane tips over in the direction of one wingtip and continues around until it is upright again

rolling turn—a maneuver in which the airplane turns in a circle and rolls at the same time

rudder—the movable control surface at the rear of the upright part of the tail which makes the airplane turn to the right or the left

sequence—the order of a series of maneuvers required in contest flying

snap roll—a particularly violent type of roll

spin—a maneuver in which the airplane slows so much that the nose suddenly drops down and the airplane tips over on one side at the same time. It then spirals down until the spin is stopped

Sukhoi—an aerobatic monoplane built in the Soviet Union which was revealed in the 1986 World Championships

tailslide—a maneuver in which the airplane flies straight up until it stops and then briefly slides backward

titanium—a rare, special kind of metal that is strong and expensive

Unknown sequence—the third stage in an aerobatic contest, in which the series of maneuvers is revealed to the pilots after the start of the contest

Zlin—a series of aerobatic monoplanes built in Czechoslovakia and flown by many countries

Index

From left to right: (front row) *Bill Thomas, Bob Tiberg, Ray Williams, Eoin Harvey, Paul Erdman, Terry Capeheart, Bill McIntyre, Bill Hunter, Bob Davis,* (back row) *Pete Anderson, Clint McHenry, Debby Rihn, Julie Pfile, Harold Chappell, Henry Haigh, Kermit Weeks, Linda Meyers, Patty Wagstaff, Gene Beggs, Bob Carmichael.*

ABOUT THE AUTHOR

Aviation and science writer Don Berliner attended the National Air Races in Cleveland (OH) for the first time in 1947. As an official in airplane racing, aerobatics contests, and world-record attempts, he has since participated in aviation events throughout the world, including EAA fly-ins in Milwaukee (WI), Rockford (IL), and Oshkosh (WI); the Reno (NV) Air Races; the Paris (France) Air Show; and World Aerobatic Championships in England, France, the U.S.S.R., Czechoslovakia, and Hungary. Author of more than one dozen books and hundreds of magazine articles about aviation, Berliner also edits the bi-monthly newsletter of the Society of Air Racing Historians. Berliner is a member of the Experimental Aircraft Association, the International Aerobatic Club, the U.S. Air Racing Association, and the International Association of Aviation Historians. He lives in Alexandria, Virginia, a suburb of Washington, D.C.